Contents

"Emotionally Empowered: A Lifelong Journey to Mental Wellness" By: Eric Wilkerson

<u>For Educational Purposes Only!</u>

<u>Introduction</u>
<u>Dedication</u>

Introduction:

Welcome to "Emotionally Empowered: A Lifelong Journey to Mental Wellness." In the pages that follow, we embark on a profound exploration of the intricate tapestry of our mental health, guided by the wisdom that understanding our emotions is the first step towards a life of enduring happiness and well-being.

In this comprehensive guide, we will navigate the diverse landscapes of emotions, delve into the core principles of mental health, and discover how the two intertwine to shape our lives. Together, we'll embark on a transformative journey, understanding the rich palette of emotions that color our world and the pivotal role they play in our mental well-being.

Drawing from scientific insights, personal stories, and practical strategies, we'll learn how good mental health isn't just an aspiration; it's an achievable reality for all of us. We'll uncover the characteristics of emotions, from their intensity to their triggers, and understand how emotional intelligence empowers us to navigate life's challenges with grace.

As we journey through these chapters, we'll explore the consequences of ignoring our mental health and how nurturing it can lead to a life of resilience, fulfillment, and emotional empowerment. We'll discuss strategies for maintaining good mental health, both individually and collectively, and advocate for mental health awareness in schools and communities.

So, whether you're a curious student, a loving parent, a dedicated teacher, or simply someone on a quest for self-improvement, this guide is designed to be your companion on the path to emotional empowerment. Together, we'll embrace our minds, cultivate resilience, and uncover the happiness that lies within, making each day a step closer to mental wellness and a life well-lived.

Dedication:

This book is dedicated to mental health awareness.

"Emotionally Empowered: A Lifelong Journey to Mental Wellness" By: Eric Wilkerson

Chapter 1: Introduction to Mental Health

In Chapter 1, we'll embark on a journey to explore the vast realm of mental health. We start by defining mental health, which encompasses emotional, psychological, and social well-being. It's the harmony within ourselves that affects how we navigate life's challenges, connect with others, and make decisions.

Characteristics of Emotions: Before we dive in, it's essential to understand that emotions are an integral part of mental health. They're our complex, subjective responses to stimuli, involving physiological, cognitive, and behavioral elements. Emotions have characteristics such as intensity, duration, valence (positive or negative), and specific triggers. This understanding sets the stage for our exploration of mental health.

Chapter 2: Understanding Emotions

Chapter 2 is a deep dive into the emotional ocean. We explore emotions' definition, emphasizing that they're our rich and colorful responses to the world around us. We feel happiness when something delightful happens and experience anger when faced with injustice.

Characteristics of Emotions: Within this chapter, we also examine the characteristics of emotions in detail. Emotions vary in intensity—some are subtle while others are intense. They can last for a moment or linger for days. Emotions can be positive, like joy or love, or negative, like fear or sadness. Additionally, they have triggers, specific events or situations that evoke them.

Chapter 3: The Importance of Mental Health

In Chapter 3, we uncover why mental health is worth our attention. Mental health isn't just about feeling good; it's about being emotionally resilient, managing stress, maintaining relationships, and making sound life choices. But why should we care?

Definition of Emotional Resilience: We'll introduce the concept of emotional resilience, the ability to bounce back from adversity and stress while maintaining mental well-being. This characteristic of mental health is vital in our understanding of why we should prioritize it.

Chapter 4 focuses on what we all aspire to achieve: good mental health. This chapter examines the characteristics of good mental health, emphasizing emotional stability, self-acceptance, and resilience.

Definition of Self-Acceptance: Self-acceptance, a crucial aspect of good mental health, is defined as having a positive view of oneself, including strengths and weaknesses, without excessive self-criticism. It's about embracing who we are, warts and all.

Chapter 5: Bad Mental Health

In Chapter 5, we confront the flip side: bad mental health. We provide a comprehensive guide to recognizing the signs and symptoms of poor mental health, including prolonged sadness, anxiety, and social withdrawal.

Definition of Emotional Dysregulation: Emotional dysregulation, a characteristic of bad mental health, refers to difficulty in managing and controlling emotional responses, often resulting in extreme reactions. Understanding this characteristic helps us identify when our mental health may be at risk.

Chapter 6: The Impact on Communities

Mental health isn't just an individual concern; it affects entire communities. In Chapter 6, we explore how various communities may be disproportionately affected by mental health challenges due to factors like access to resources and cultural stigmas.

Definition of Cultural Stigma: Cultural stigma, an important concept in this chapter, refers to negative attitudes, beliefs, and stereotypes surrounding mental health within specific cultural or social groups. It helps us understand why some communities may face unique challenges in addressing mental health.

Chapter 7 serves as a stark reminder of the consequences of neglecting mental health. We delve into the potential fallout, including physical health problems, strained relationships, and a diminished quality of life.

Definition of Emotional Neglect: Emotional neglect, a characteristic of ignoring mental health, occurs when an individual's emotional needs are consistently unmet, leading to emotional distress and potential mental health issues. Recognizing emotional neglect helps us understand the risks of neglecting our emotional well-being.

Chapter 8: Coping Strategies

Chapter 8 equips readers with a toolkit of healthy coping strategies. We explore how activities like exercise, mindfulness, and seeking professional help can be powerful tools for managing stress and improving mental well-being.

Definition of Mindfulness: Mindfulness is a mental practice that involves staying fully present and aware of the current moment without judgment. This characteristic of good mental health is especially relevant in this chapter as we discuss its practical applications for managing emotions and reducing stress.

Chapter 9: Mental Health Awareness in Schools

Now, let's shift our focus to schools in Chapter 9. We emphasize the importance of nurturing emotional intelligence in educational settings.

Definition of Emotional Intelligence: Emotional intelligence is the ability to recognize, understand, manage, and effectively use one's own emotions and those of others. We'll discuss how emotional intelligence contributes to healthier relationships, better decision-making, and improved mental well-being, all within the context of schools.

Chapter 10: Promoting Mental Wellness for All Ages

In our final chapter, we tie it all together. We revisit the characteristics of emotions, emphasizing how understanding and managing them can be a lifelong journey towards mental wellness. Our catchy jingle title, "Embrace Your Mind: A Guide to Happiness You'll Find," resonates as a reminder of the importance of emotional well-being for individuals of all ages.

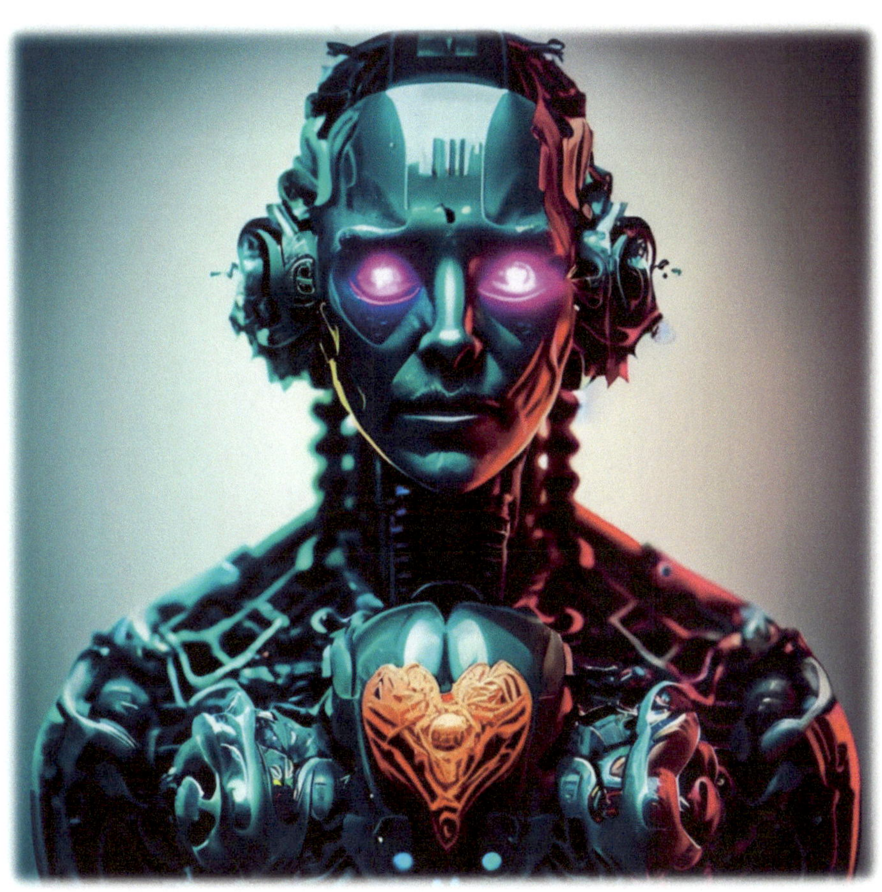

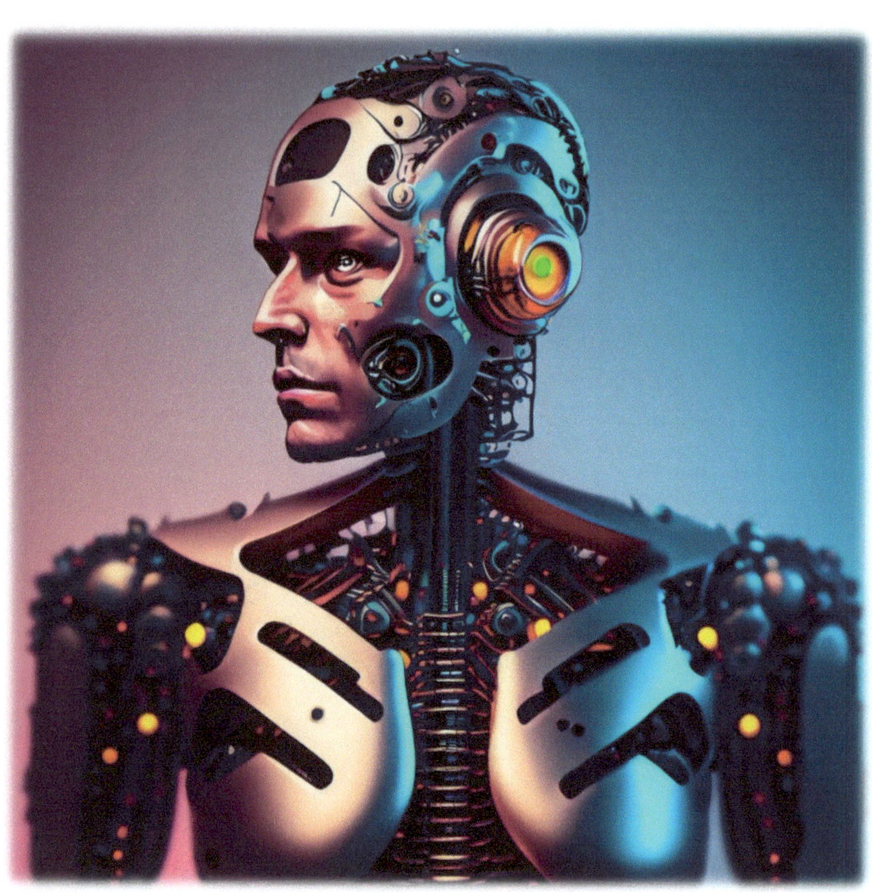

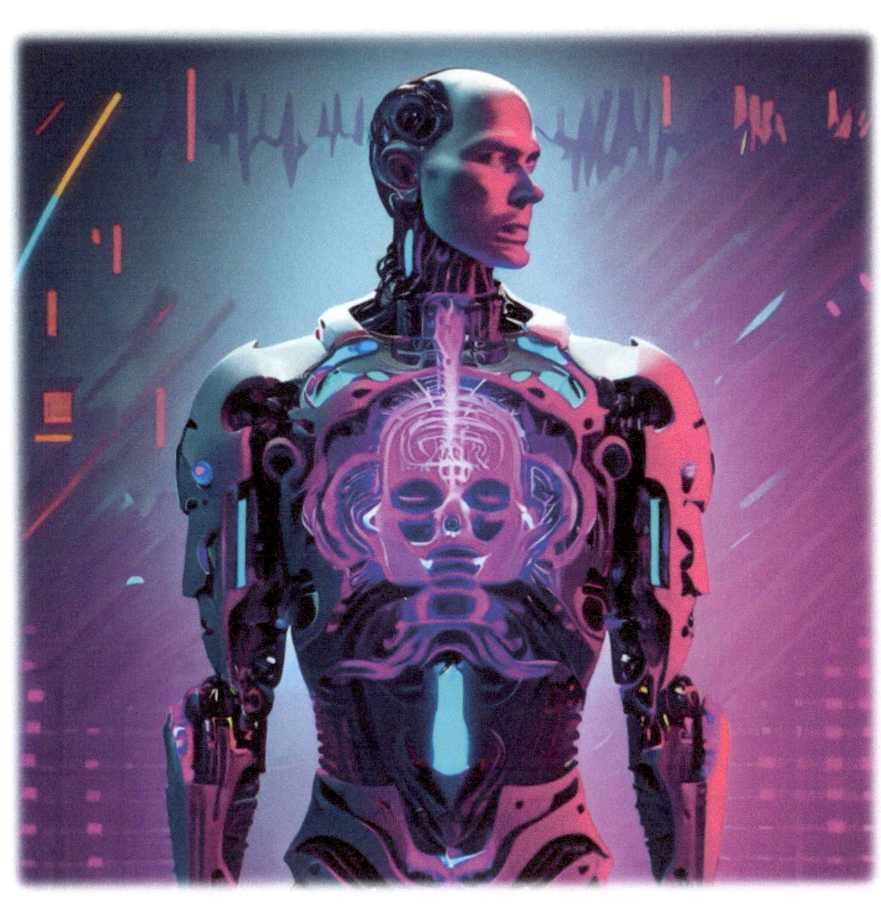

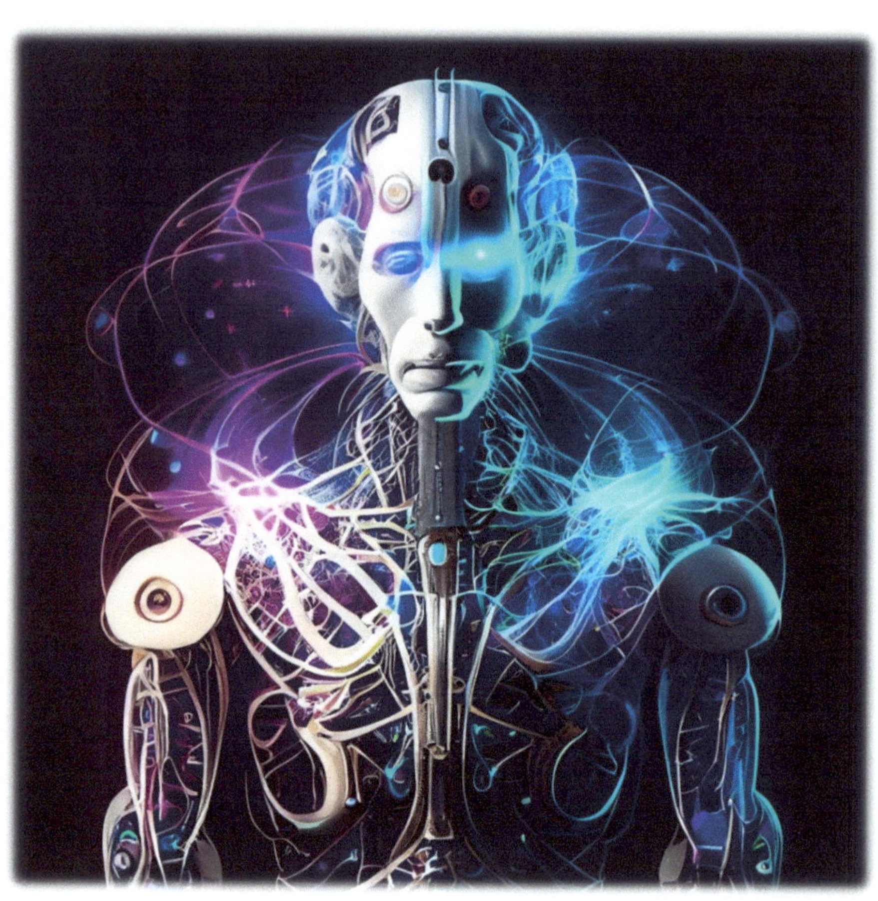